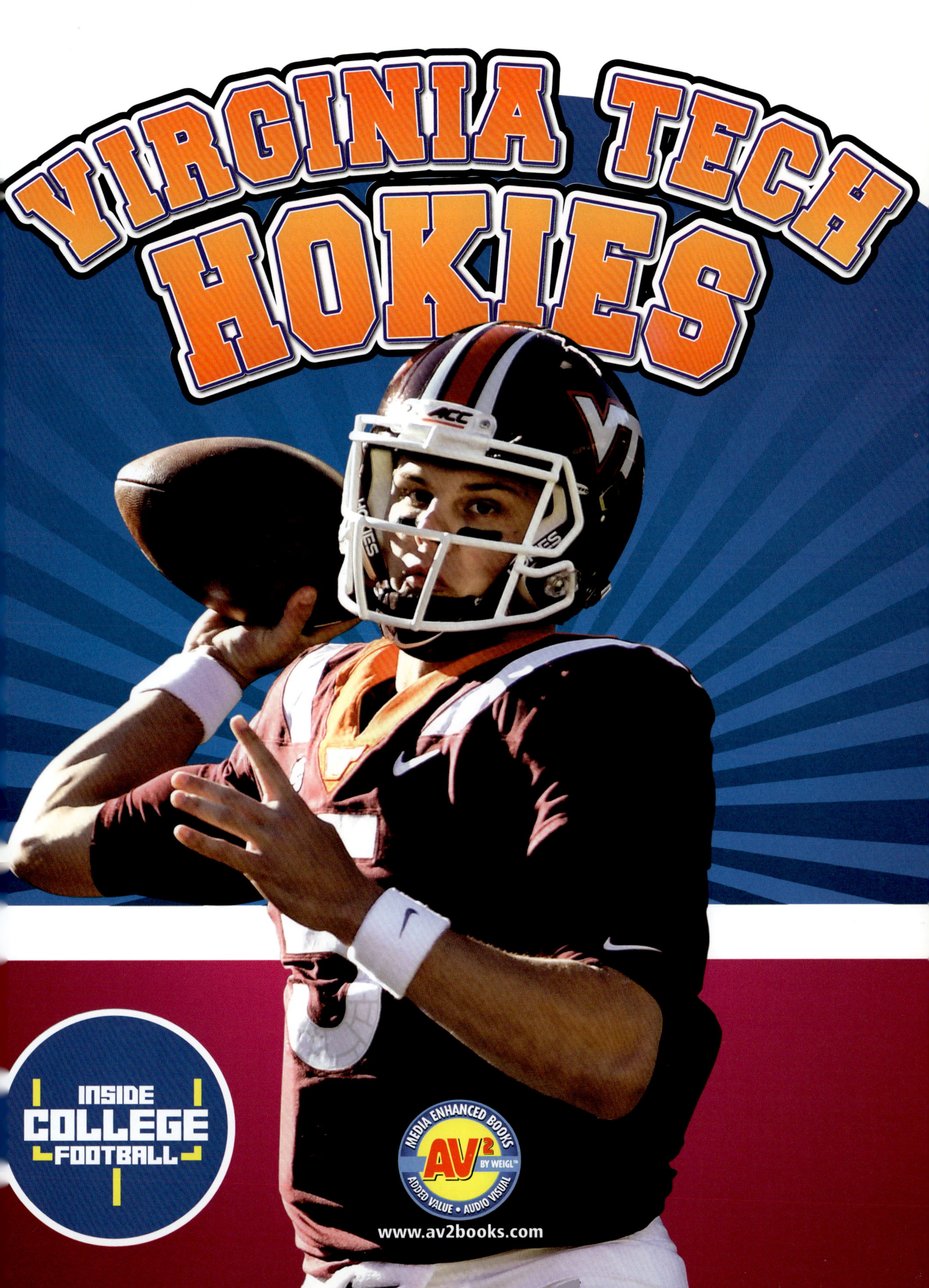
VIRGINIA TECH
HOKIES
INSIDE
COLLEGE
FOOTBALL
MEDIA ENHANCED BOOKS
AV2
BY WEIGL
ADDED VALUE • AUDIO VISUAL
www.av2books.com

Go to www.av2books.com, and enter this book's unique code.

BOOK CODE

AVZ96632

AV² by Weigl brings you media enhanced books that support active learning.

AV² provides enriched content that supplements and complements this book. Weigl's AV² books strive to create inspired learning and engage young minds in a total learning experience.

Your AV² Media Enhanced books come alive with...

Audio
Listen to sections of the book read aloud.

Video
Watch informative video clips.

Embedded Weblinks
Gain additional information for research.

Try This!
Complete activities and hands-on experiments.

Key Words
Study vocabulary, and complete a matching word activity.

Quizzes
Test your knowledge.

Slideshow
View images and captions, and prepare a presentation.

... and much, much more!

Published by AV² by Weigl
350 5th Avenue, 59th Floor
New York, NY 10118
Website: www.av2books.com

Library of Congress Control Number: 2018968217

ISBN 978-1-7911-0129-9 (hardcover)
ISBN 978-1-7911-0130-5 (multi-user eBook)
ISBN 978-1-7911-0131-2 (single-user eBook)

Printed in Guangzhou, China
1 2 3 4 5 6 7 8 9 0 23 22 21 20 19

042019
102318

Project Coordinator: Jared Siemens   Designer: Terry Paulhus

The publisher acknowledges Alamy, Flickr CC, Getty Images, and Wikimedia Commons as its primary image suppliers for this title.

Virginia Tech Hokies

CONTENTS

Introduction

The Hokies are the football team for Virginia Tech (VT). Also known as Tech, the school is officially named Virginia Polytechnic Institute and State University. The Hokies have been part of the National Collegiate Athletic Association (NCAA) Atlantic Coast Conference, or ACC, since 2004. Virginia Tech previously played in the Big East Conference. The team has an incredible 744–472–46 record across 125 seasons.

The Hokies hold 11 conference titles. Their most recent is from 2010. They are tied with Clemson University and Florida State University for the most titles of any ACC team since they joined in 2004. Since 1970, Tech has more number-one overall **draft** picks in the National Football League (NFL) Draft than any other current ACC teams.

Alongside its strong playing record, the team's culture is rich with history. One cherished tradition includes the team's entrance before games. When the team emerges onto the field at Lane Stadium, "Enter Sandman" by Metallica plays. The intensity of this notorious entrance is very intimidating to opponents.

Dalton Keene joined Virginia Tech in 2017 as a tight end and logged more than 160 yards in his first six games with the Hokies.

In his four seasons with the Hokies from 2015 to 2018, running back Steven Peoples had 13 touchdowns and 1,414 total yards for Virginia Tech.

VIRGINIA TECH

Stadium Lane Stadium

Division Atlantic Coast Conference (ACC) Coastal

Head Coach Justin Fuente

Location Blacksburg, Virginia

National Championships 0

Nicknames Hokies

4 ACC Championships

88 Winning Seasons

22 Hokies Currently in the NFL

55 Undefeated Seasons at Home

History

The **Lunch Pail** contains the names of the 32 Hokies who died in the mass shooting at Virginia Tech on April 16, 2007.

After retiring from his head coaching position, legendary coach Frank Beamer became the special assistant to Virginia Tech's director of athletics. Beamer was also appointed to the College Football Playoff Selection Committee.

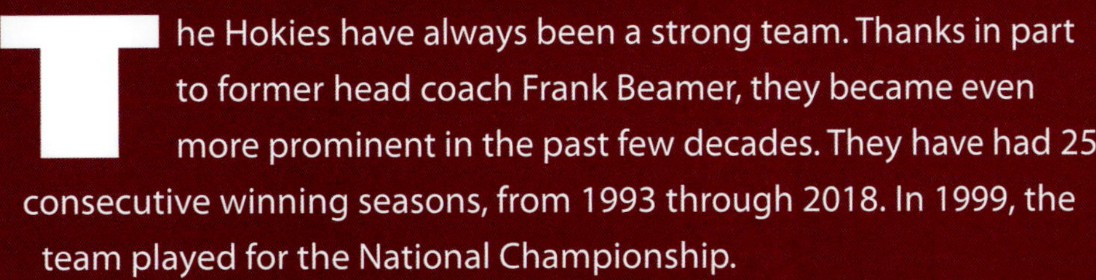

The Hokies have always been a strong team. Thanks in part to former head coach Frank Beamer, they became even more prominent in the past few decades. They have had 25 consecutive winning seasons, from 1993 through 2018. In 1999, the team played for the National Championship.

Under Beamer, the Hokies became famous for a style of play called Beamer Ball. Beamer encouraged the entire team, even defense and special teams, to score. During Beamer's time, 55 touchdowns were scored by special teams, a rare occurrence in college football.

Another recent but cherished tradition is the Lunch Pail. Since 1995, this pail travels with the defense. It holds a mission statement signed by each defensive player. The pail represents defensive coordinator Bud Foster's tough, blue-collar approach to defense. It also represents the team's blue-collar mining heritage.

A key part of the team's history is its **rivalry** with the Virginia Cavaliers of the University of Virginia (UVA). It is called the Commonwealth Cup, and it has been played 100 times since 1895. Tech has won 15 years straight, from 2004 to 2018. One notable game was after the Virginia Tech mass shooting in 2007. The teams had identical records, and they were playing for a chance at the championship. UVA showed love and support for Tech's tragedy.

The lunch pail, which once belonged to a coal miner, is entrusted to a member of the team's defense each week.

The Stadium

The playing surface of Lane Stadium is called Worsham Field after longtime Hokies supporter Wes Worsham, who helped fund multiple stadium renovations in the early 1990s.

The Hokies played at Miles Stadium until 1965. Their first game at their current home, Lane Stadium, was against the College of William and Mary Tribe on October 2, 1965. Construction was not finished until 1969. The capacity of Lane Stadium has been 65,632 since 2003.

Lane Stadium is one of the loudest stadiums in college football. The enclosed south end zone is particularly loud. This is one reason the stadium is considered the number-one toughest place for opponents to play. It is also why the Hokies have one of the best home-field advantages in college football. Their record at home is 55–10 since 2004.

The stadium has many high-tech features. A "HokieVision" video scoreboard was added in 2013. It is the third-largest scoreboard in college football. The stadium crew needs five cameras, four replay machines, and 10 editing stations to operate it. Practice can be filmed with **virtual reality** cameras as a learning tool for players. They can wear goggles to "go inside" previously-filmed practices. Players also use the Beamer-Lawson Indoor Practice Facility. It is the length of two jets, and it features a half-acre of grass.

Lane Stadium's "HokieVision" scoreboard is nearly five times larger than its previous board. It measures 48 feet (15 meters) high by 108 feet (33 m) wide.

Where They Play

Welcome to Lane Stadium, home of the Virginia Tech Hokies. Located in the mountains of Virginia, it is one of the loudest and most intimidating stadiums in college football. The stadium is a sea of orange and maroon when fans fill the stands to watch the Hokies play.

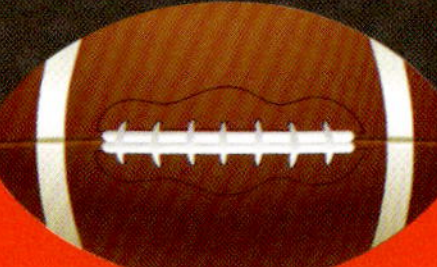

ACC ATLANTIC

1. **Boston College**
   Chestnut Hill, Massachusetts
2. **Clemson University**
   Clemson, South Carolina
3. **Florida State University**
   Tallahassee, Florida
4. **North Carolina State University**
   Raleigh, North Carolina
5. **Syracuse University**
   Syracuse, New York
6. **University of Louisville**
   Louisville, Kentucky
7. **University of Notre Dame**
   Notre Dame, Indiana
8. **Wake Forest University**
   Winston-Salem, North Carolina

Arena
Lane Stadium

Location
Blacksburg, Virginia

Broke Ground
1964

Completed
1969

Surface
Real Grass

Features

- Virginia Tech Sports **Hall of Fame** Museum located on the west side of the stadium
- A bronze statue of Frank Beamer stands in Moody Plaza, outside of the stadium
- Hokie Stone, a local limestone rock mined by the university, is on the walls of each end zone

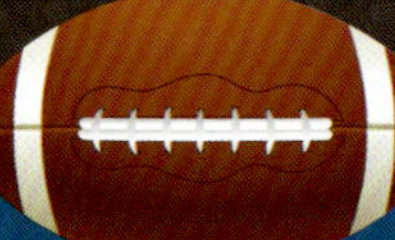

ACC COASTAL

1. **Duke University**
   Durham, North Carolina
2. **Georgia Institute of Technology**
   Atlanta, Georgia
3. **University of Miami**
   Coral Gables, Florida
4. **University of North Carolina at Chapel Hill**
   Chapel Hill, North Carolina
5. **University of Pittsburgh**
   Pittsburgh, Pennsylvania
6. **University of Virginia**
   Charlottesville, Virginia
7. ★ **Virginia Polytechnic Institute and State University**
   Blacksburg, Virginia

NORTH DAKOTA
SOUTH DAKOTA
MINNESOTA
WISCONSIN
MICHIGAN
IOWA
NEBRASKA
ILLINOIS
INDIANA
OHIO
KANSAS
MISSOURI
KENTUCKY
WEST VIRGINIA
VIRGINIA
PENNSYLVANIA
NEW YORK
MAINE
NEW HAMPSHIRE
VERMONT
MASSACHUSETTS
RHODE ISLAND
CONNECTICUT
NEW JERSEY
DELAWARE
MARYLAND
WASHINGTON, D.C.
NORTH CAROLINA
TENNESSEE
SOUTH CAROLINA
OKLAHOMA
ARKANSAS
MISSISSIPPI
ALABAMA
GEORGIA
TEXAS
LOUISIANA
FLORIDA
Atlantic Ocean
Gulf of Mexico
LEGEND
Home Stadium
ACC Atlantic
ACC Coastal
United States
Other Countries
Water
SCALE
0 miles
500 miles
0 kilometers
500 km

The Uniforms

In 2014 and 2017, for **Military Appreciation Day**, the Hokies' solid white helmets featured the Virginia Tech logo with an **American flag** background and a white-blue-red stripe.

Virginia Tech has partnered with Nike since 2006 to create uniforms for the Hokies. Nike also provides shoes, socks, gloves, and practice uniforms as part of the agreement.

Virginia Tech's colors are burnt orange and maroon. These colors were chosen in 1896 because the original colors of black and gray were not bright enough. The first time the school wore the colors was against the Roanoke College Maroons on October 26, 1896.

Current uniforms have solid-colored pants and jerseys with angled white shoulder stripes. Jersey numbers have a Hokie Stone pattern. An alternate black uniform with gray Hokie Stone shoulder patches was introduced in 2018. Since the team's first colors were black and gray, incorporating these colors is a nod to the team's history.

The team has worn more than 50 different helmet designs since 1987. One notable helmet was a Hokie Stone-patterned helmet with the Virginia Tech shield. Others were helmets with an orange "digital camouflage" pattern, and helmets adorned with bird tracks, a connection to the team mascot. Current helmets are maroon or white with an orange center stripe.

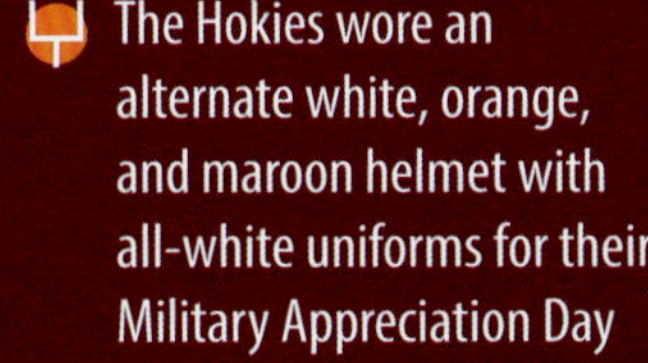

The Hokies wore an alternate white, orange, and maroon helmet with all-white uniforms for their Military Appreciation Day game in 2015.

Student Athletes

Beginning in 2017, season ticket holders seated in **"scholarship sections"** at Lane Stadium contribute a per-seat scholarship gift each year.

Virginia Tech's starting defensive line was made up of mostly freshmen and sophomores during the 2018 season. Young players like freshman Dax Hollifield and sophomore Bryce Watts brought new energy to the team and gained valuable experience for future seasons.

Being a college student athlete is hard work. Student athletes have to perform well on the football field and in the classroom. Virginia Tech student athletes are required to meet a minimum grade point average to remain eligible to play. Student athletes meet these expectations with the help of Student Athlete Academic Support Services. The Office of Student Athlete Support Services offers many other services to help them balance the student athlete life.

Many student athletes are given athletic scholarships. An athletic scholarship is a financial aid agreement between the athlete and the college or university. Athletes who do not receive an athletic scholarship can be "walk-on" members of the team. This means they are on the team, but without athletic financial aid. Virginia Tech typically awards the maximum number of football scholarships allowed, which is 85.

Sophomore wide receiver Hezekiah Grimsley joined the Hokies in 2017 as one of Tech's 85 football scholarship recipients. Grimsley played in 11 games for the Hokies during the 2018 season, logging 457 total yards and two touchdowns.

Bowl Games

The **biggest comeback** in Hokies history was against the University of **Arkansas Razorbacks** in the Belk Bowl in 2016. Down 24–0 at the end of the first half, Tech won 35–24.

The Hokies entered the 2014 Military Bowl with a 6–6 record and were not favored to win, but they defeated the University of Cincinnati Bearcats 33–17.

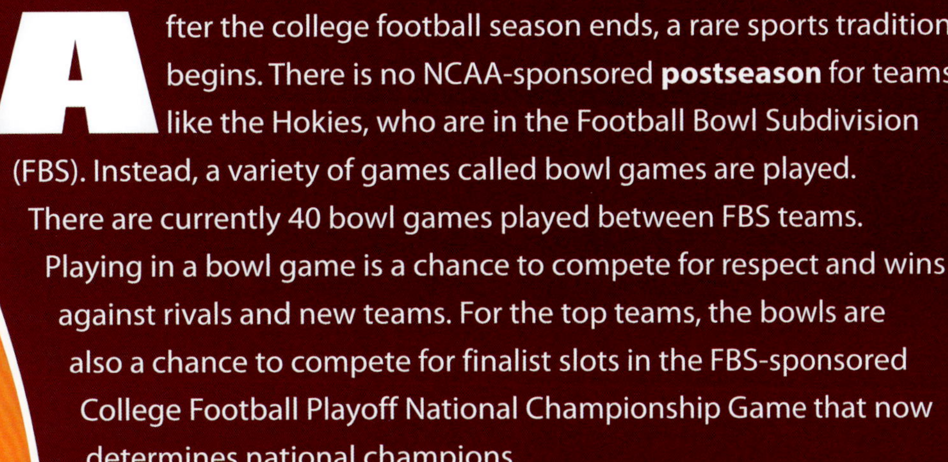

After the college football season ends, a rare sports tradition begins. There is no NCAA-sponsored **postseason** for teams like the Hokies, who are in the Football Bowl Subdivision (FBS). Instead, a variety of games called bowl games are played. There are currently 40 bowl games played between FBS teams. Playing in a bowl game is a chance to compete for respect and wins against rivals and new teams. For the top teams, the bowls are also a chance to compete for finalist slots in the FBS-sponsored College Football Playoff National Championship Game that now determines national champions.

The Hokies have a 13–19 bowl record. They have played 26-straight bowls, and are tied with the University of Alabama Crimson Tide for the third-longest streak in college football history. Virginia Tech's first postseason bowl game was in 1947, in the Sun Bowl against the Cincinnati Bearcats. Tech had three consecutive bowl wins from 2014 to 2016.

The Hokies have played the Cincinnati Bearcats 12 times since 1947, most recently in the 2018 Military Bowl. The teams are tied for wins and losses against each other, with six each.

The Coaches

Frank Beamer won seven titles in two conferences. He led the Hokies to victory in the Big East Conference in 1995, 1996, and 1999, and in the ACC in 2004, 2007, 2008, and 2010.

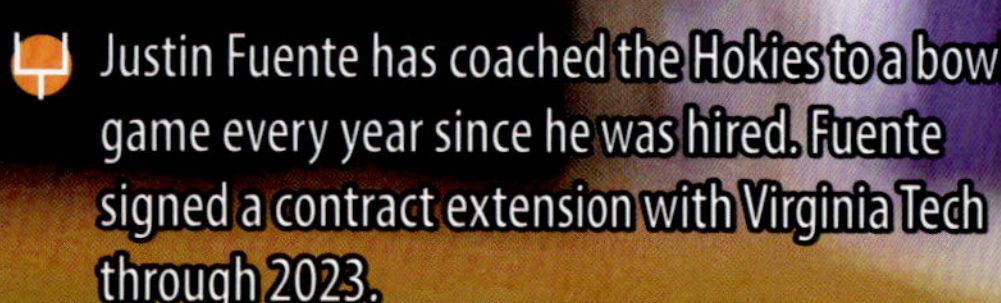

Justin Fuente has coached the Hokies to a bowl game every year since he was hired. Fuente signed a contract extension with Virginia Tech through 2023.

The Hokies have played under 34 different head coaches. The **offensive** success of Beamer Ball continues under current head coach Justin Fuente. Hokies coaches are also known for creating defensive **dominance**. Defensive coordinator Bud Foster created the Lunch Pail Defense, which emphasizes grit and hard work. The Hokies defense is among the best in the country under Foster. Foster is only one of the many assistant coaches who have helped Tech develop a history of dominance.

JERRY CLAIBORNE Jerry Claiborne coached the Hokies from 1961 to 1970. When he retired, he was the school's winningest coach, with a 61–39–2 record. He is a member of the College Football Hall of Fame. Claiborne was also known for classroom stars, with four Academic All-Americans and 87 players on the Southeastern Conference All-Academic team.

FRANK BEAMER Frank Beamer is Tech's winningest coach. From 1987 to 2015, Beamer had 280 victories. With his signature Beamer Ball, he took the Hokies to 23 consecutive bowl games. This included the National Championship game in 1999. Beamer retired after 29 seasons at Virginia Tech. He was inducted into the College Football Hall of Fame in 2018.

JUSTIN FUENTE Justin Fuente has coached two winning seasons since being named head coach of Virginia Tech in 2016. This includes one impressive 10-win season. He boasts the most wins by any Tech coach in his first two seasons, with 19. Fuente was named the 2016 ACC Coach of the Year and the 2016 top first-year FBS head coach in the nation.

The Mascot

After every score in a VT football game, the HokieBird does a bench press on the sideline for every point the Hokies have scored.

Until the 1970s, "Hokies" and "Gobblers" were both used as team nicknames before a coach insisted on dropping Gobblers. Hokie was a meaningless word from a spirit chant. The school legend is that Gobblers was chosen because of how much student athletes ate. Originally, the mascot was a turkey. However, a less turkey-like bird mascot was created when the team became the Hokies. It was named the HokieBird.

Four students alternate playing the mascot each season. The HokieBird costume has huge orange feet, a padded vest, large hands, and a bird-shaped head with a helmet inside. Students who dress as the HokieBird are anonymous until commencement. On graduation day, they wear the feet into Lane Stadium as they walk across the stage.

In 1981, VT art student George Wills helped the athletic department design an updated mascot for the Hokies. Five years later in 1986, when the mascot needed another update, Wills, who was working as an illustrator and cartoonist in Blacksburg, designed the HokieBird that Virginia Tech fans know and love today.

Legends of the Past

For many players, their time with the Hokies is the start of a promising football career. These are some of the best-known football players to play for Virginia Tech.

Bruce Smith

Bruce Smith was a consensus All-American. He ended his Tech career by winning the Outland Trophy as America's top lineman. Known as "The Sack Man" of Tech football, Smith had 46 career quarterback sacks at Tech. He was the 1985 number-one overall pick by the Buffalo Bills. He was named Associated Press Defensive Player of the Year twice. He played in 11 **Pro Bowls** and in the **Super Bowl** 4 times. Smith is the NFL all-time sack leader with 200 sacks. He became a member of the Pro Football Hall of Fame in 2009. Smith ended his NFL career in 2003.

Position: Defensive Lineman
Seasons: 1981–1984 (Virginia Tech Hokies), 1985–1999 (Buffalo Bills), 2000–2003 (Washington Redskins)
Born: June 18, 1963, Norfolk, Virginia

Duane Brown

Duane Brown started as a tight end for the Hokies in 2004. A talented and versatile athlete, he switched to offensive tackle in 2005. He started every Hokies game after that. In 2006, Brown had 22 pass deflections. He received second team All-ACC and state Offensive Lineman/End of the Year honors after two different seasons. Brown was a first-round draft pick in 2008 and has started more than 150 NFL games. He is a four-time Pro Bowl pick and was first-team All-Pro in 2012. Brown currently plays for the Seattle Seahawks.

Position: Offensive Tackle
Seasons: 2004–2007 (Virginia Tech Hokies), 2008–2017 (Houston Texans), 2017–Present (Seattle Seahawks)
Born: August 30, 1985, Richmond, Virginia

Kam Chancellor

Kam Chancellor was one of the hardest hitters in college football and the NFL. He changed positions several times when he started at Tech in 2006. Chancellor had 68 tackles as a senior. He was a fifth-round draft pick in 2010 by the Seahawks. He was a four-time Pro Bowl selection. Chancellor won a Super Bowl ring in 2014 as part of the well-known Legion of Boom defense. In the 2014 Super Bowl, he played extremely well, even intercepting Peyton Manning. He was on track to be one of the best in the NFL, but a 2017 injury placed Chancellor on the Seahawks' injured reserve list indefinitely, even though he is still a member of the team.

Position: Safety
Seasons: 2006–2009 (Virginia Tech Hokies), 2010–Present (Seattle Seahawks)
Born: April 3, 1988, Norfolk, Virginia

DeAngelo Hall

DeAngelo Hall is one of few players in college football to ever score on offense, defense, and special teams. At Virginia Tech, his five returns for touchdowns rank second in Big East history. In his junior year, Hall set a Tech and Big East record with two punt returns for touchdowns. Hall was drafted eighth overall in the first round of the 2004 draft. He is a three-time Pro Bowl pick and was named the 2010 Pro Bowl **Most Valuable Player (MVP)**. He also scored five touchdowns in his career, an uncommon statistic for defensive players. Hall retired after the 2017 season.

Position: Defensive Back
Seasons: 2001–2003 (Virginia Tech Hokies), 2004–2007 (Atlanta Falcons), 2008 (Oakland Raiders), 2008–2017 (Washington Redskins)
Born: November 19, 1983, Chesapeake, Virginia

All-Time Records

27

Consecutive Games with a Touchdown

Lee Suggs set the NCAA record for most consecutive games scoring a touchdown, with 27 games from 2001 to 2003.

78

Career Field Goals Made

During his four seasons with the Hokies, from 2014 to 2017, Joey Slye made 78 career field goals, a Virginia Tech record.

455

Most Points in a Season

The most points scored by any Virginia Tech football team in a season was 455 points in 1999.

5

Most Touchdowns on Returns

DeAngelo Hall scored the most touchdowns on returns in a Virginia Tech player's college career, with five from 2001 to 2003.

10,362

Most Yards in a Career

From 2010 to 2013, quarterback Logan Thomas logged a record 10,362 career yards, the most in Hokies history.

Timeline

Throughout the team's history, the Virginia Tech Hokies have had many memorable events that have become defining moments for the team and its fans.

1892
Virginia Agricultural and Mechanical College is victorious in its first game ever. The school does not become Virginia Polytechnic Institute until 1896.

In 1896, maroon and orange are first worn in a football game against Roanoke College. The same year, a contest is held for a new school chant and O. M. Stull wins for his "Old Hokie."

1918
Tech plays its first undefeated regular season, with a 7–0–0 record.

1926
Tech's first homecoming football game is played against the University of Virginia at the dedication of Miles Stadium. Virginia Tech wins the game 6–0.

1947
Tech's first bowl game is the Sun Bowl in El Paso, Texas, where the team loses to Cincinnati 6–18.

1963
The then-Gobblers win Tech's only outright Southern Conference title.

1900 | 1920 | 1940 | 1960

The Future
The recruiting class when Coach Fuente entered was only ranked 42 in the FBS. The 2017 class was ranked 26th, and 2018's was ranked 24th. This increasingly strong pool of players creates depth for Virginia Tech. The team is full of young players ready to take the Hokies back to national prominence.

1986
Legendary coach Frank Beamer is hired.

2000
Ending one of their greatest seasons at the Sugar Bowl, the Hokies lose the National Championship to Florida State University 29–46 after leading at the end of the third quarter.

1980

2000

2020

In 1995, the team wins its biggest victory yet, coming from behind to defeat Texas, 28–10, in the Sugar Bowl in New Orleans. The season ends 10–2 and the Hokies finish their highest ever in the polls.

2017
The Hokies finish the 2017 season ranked 24th in the nation, with nine wins and a spot in the school's 25th consecutive bowl game since 1993.

1999
The Hokies have their finest season, during which they go undefeated and are ranked second in the nation, the highest ever for the team.

Write a Biography

Life Story

A person's life story can be the subject of a book. This kind of book is called a biography. Biographies often describe the lives of people who have achieved great success. These people may be alive today, or they may have lived many years ago. Reading a biography can help you learn more about a great person.

Get the Facts

Use this book, and research in the library and on the internet, to find out more about your favorite player. Learn as much about him as you can. What position does he play? What are his statistics in important categories? Has he set any records? Also, be sure to write down key events in the person's life. What was his childhood like? What has he accomplished off the field? Is there anything else that makes this person special or unusual?

Use the Concept Web

A concept web is a useful research tool. Read the questions in the concept web on the following page. Answer the questions in your notebook. Your answers will help you write a biography.

Concept Web

Adulthood
- Where does this individual currently reside?
- Does he have a family?

Your Opinion
- What did you learn from the books you read in your research?
- Would you suggest these books to others?
- Was anything missing from these books?

Childhood
- Where and when was this person born?
- Describe his parents, siblings, and friends.
- Did this person grow up in unusual circumstances?

Write a Biography

Accomplishments off the Field
- What is this person's life's work?
- Has he received awards or recognition for accomplishments?
- How have this person's accomplishments served others?

Help and Obstacles
- Did this individual have a positive attitude?
- Did he receive help from others?
- Did this person have a mentor?
- Did this person face any hardships?
- If so, how were the hardships overcome?

Accomplishments on the Field
- What records does this person hold?
- What key games and plays have defined his career?
- What are his stats in categories important to his position?

Work and Preparation
- What was this person's education?
- What was his work experience?
- How does this person work?
- What is the process he uses?

Trivia Time

Take this quiz to test your knowledge of the Virginia Tech Hokies. The answers are printed upside down under each question.

1 What is the name of the team's defensive strategy?

A. Lunch Pail Defense

2 Who does VT play for the Commonwealth Cup?

A. UVA Cavaliers

3 What nickname was eventually dropped in order to make "Hokies" Virginia Tech's official nickname?

A. The Gobblers

4 What is the name of the local stone that is used as a pattern on VT uniforms?

A. Hokie Stone

5 Which former Hokies player became a member of the Pro Football Hall of Fame?

A. Bruce Smith

6 Which team was the Hokies' largest comeback against?

A. The Arkansas Razorbacks

7 Who is the winningest football coach in VT history?

A. Frank Beamer

8 What song plays when the players take the field?

A. "Enter Sandman" by Metallica

9 What are the Hokies' colors?

A. Burnt orange and maroon

10 How many conference titles have the Hokies won?

A. 11

Key Words

dominance: holding a powerful position over others

draft: an annual event where the NFL chooses college football players to be new team members

Hall of Fame: a group of persons judged to be outstanding in a particular sport

Most Valuable Player (MVP): the player judged to be most valuable to his team's success

offensive: the action of attacking the opposite team in order to score points

postseason: a sporting event that takes place after the end of the regular season

Pro Bowls: the annual all-star games for NFL players pitting the best players in the National Football Conference against the best players in the American Football Conference

rivalry: competition between different groups or individuals toward the same objective or goal

Super Bowl: the NFL's annual championship game between the winning team from the National Football Conference and the winning team from the American Football Conference

virtual reality: a computer-generated three-dimensional environment that seems real and can be interacted with by a person wearing special electronic gear

Index

Log on to www.av2books.com

AV² by Weigl brings you media enhanced books that support active learning. Go to www.av2books.com, and enter the special code found on page 2 of this book. You will gain access to enriched and enhanced content that supplements and complements this book. Content includes video, audio, weblinks, quizzes, a slideshow, and activities.

AV² Online Navigation

Audio
Listen to sections of the book read aloud.

Book Pages
AV² pages directly correspond to pages in the book.

Video
Watch informative video clips.

Embedded Weblinks
Gain additional information for research.

Key Words
Study vocabulary, and complete a matching word activity.

Try This!
Complete activities and hands-on experiments.

Quizzes
Test your knowledge.

Slideshow
View images and captions, and prepare a presentation.

AV² was built to bridge the gap between print and digital. We encourage you to tell us what you like and what you want to see in the future.

Sign up to be an AV² Ambassador at www.av2books.com/ambassador.

Due to the dynamic nature of the internet, some of the URLs and activities provided as part of AV² by Weigl may have changed or ceased to exist. AV² by Weigl accepts no responsibility for any such changes. All media enhanced books are regularly monitored to update addresses and sites in a timely manner. Contact AV² by Weigl at 1-866-649-3445 or av2books@weigl.com with any questions, comments, or feedback.